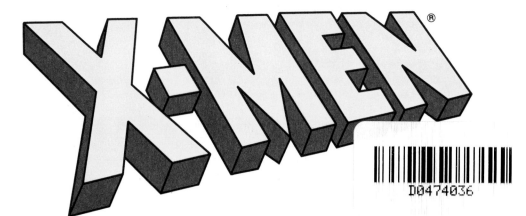

D0474036

TO STOP A JUGGERNAUT

based on a teleplay by Julianne Klemm
illustrated by Gray Morrow
cover painting by Francis Mao

Random House  New York

Cyclops called everyone to the <u>War Room</u>, located on one of the many below-ground floors of the mansion, where the <u>holographic</u> image of the Professor spoke.

I AM TAKING A JOURNEY, THE RESULTS OF WHICH MAY CHANGE THE LIVES OF MUTANTS FOREVER.

Wolverine got up and left. He aimed to find out who had trashed the mansion.

Using his <u>ultra</u>-sharp sense of smell, Wolverine was hot on the trail of the mansion's wrecker.

But Jubilee broke away and followed Wolverine to a construction site by herself! There she watched a giant <u>mutant</u> carrying on like a one-man wrecking crew!

THAT'S GOTTA BE THE GUY WHO TOTALED THE MANSION!

Making the same mistake as Jubilee, Wolverine leaped onto the giant mutant's back.

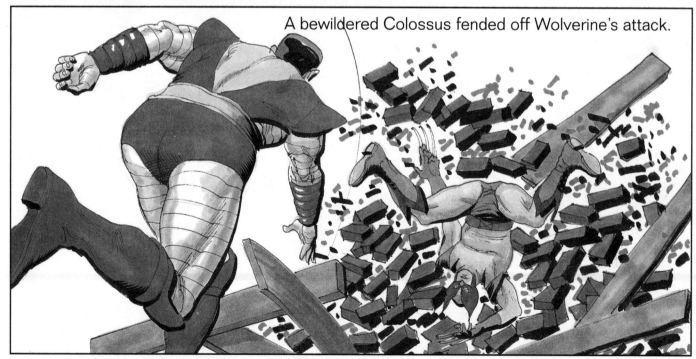

A bewildered Colossus fended off Wolverine's attack.

Later that afternoon, Wolverine and Jubilee discovered a bank had been robbed…by someone BIG.

Colossus was BIG. And he just happened to be opening an account at the time of the robbery. The police dragged him off to jail.

But Colossus didn't *stay* in jail, for Cyclops sent Rogue and Storm to the prison to <u>spring</u> the big Russian. They would free him, then prove his innocence.

But a funny thing happened on the way out of the jailhouse. They saw a fellow team member, Beast, who had been arrested on charges of crimes against the government.

Rogue went for the Juggernaut.

The mighty Colossus whirled an army tank over his head, but it merely bounced off the <u>armored</u> Juggernaut.

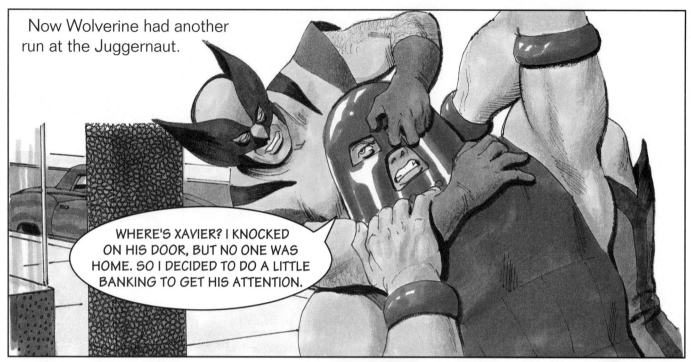

Now Wolverine had another run at the Juggernaut.

WHERE'S XAVIER? I KNOCKED ON HIS DOOR, BUT NO ONE WAS HOME. SO I DECIDED TO DO A LITTLE BANKING TO GET HIS ATTENTION.

CRASH!

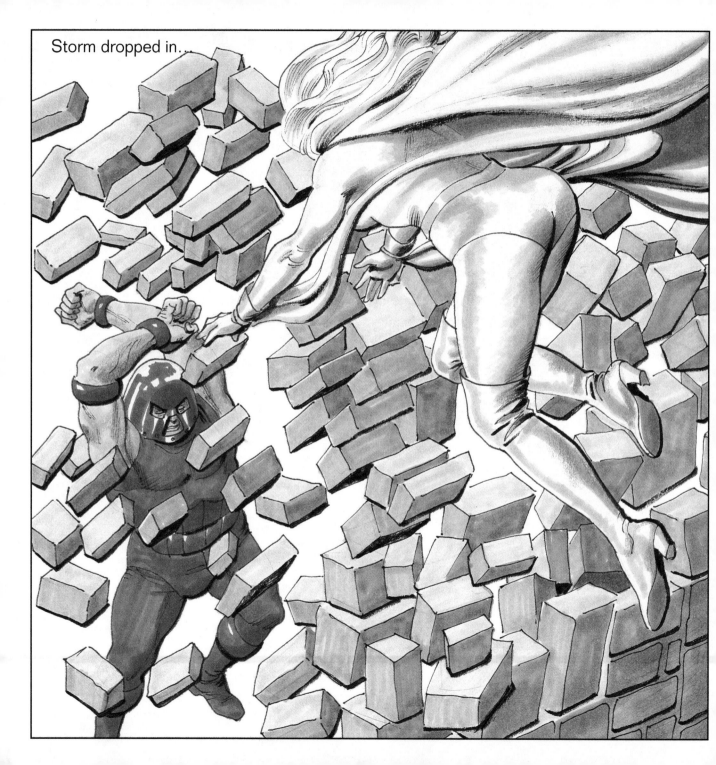
Storm dropped in...

Only with teamwork could the X-Men hope to defeat the Juggernaut. First Jubilee blasted plasmoids.

Then Cyclops let loose his <u>optic blast</u>.

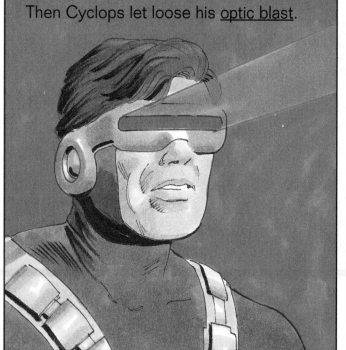

Storm drew a dark curtain of clouds around the Juggernaut, blinding him.

Colossus held his arms while Wolverine hacked at his helmet.

Finally, Rogue pried off his helmet!

Rogue laid her hand on Juggernaut's neck to absorb all his powers.

But along with the powers, she absorbed many of Juggernaut's memories! As Juggernaut's immense power <u>radiated</u> from her, she called out in Juggernaut's voice.

Juggernaut—the evil one, the menace—was none other than the stepbrother of Charles Xavier, Professor X!

Jean Grey locked onto the now <u>vulnerable</u> Juggernaut's mind.

The X-Men returned home to the mansion to clean up the mess before the Professor's return.

THIS IS THE FIRST PLACE THAT EVER REALLY FELT LIKE HOME TO ME.

GLOSSARY

armored: Protected by a hard shell, like a turtle or a tank.

faze: To confuse or startle.

hologram: A 3-dimensional projected image.

mind probe: An attempt by a telepath, like Professor X or Jean Grey, to enter someone's mind in an effort to read their thoughts or influence their actions.

mutant: A person born with abilities far beyond those of ordinary humans. A mutant can look like an average human being, or not, depending on the particular mutation. Many people are afraid of mutants and their powers.

optic blast: The force that comes from Cyclops's eyes. It can only be stopped by the visor of his costume or by special glasses made of ruby quartz.

plasmoids: Bursts of plasma (a mixture of energy and gas) such as those produced by Jubilee and released through her fingertips.

radiate: To give off in all directions, the way a light bulb radiates light or a fire radiates heat.

rampage: Violent, uncontrolled, destructive behavior.

spring: To release someone or something.

telepathy: Reading another person's mind, or communicating mind-to-mind. People who can do this are called telepaths.

ultra-: Extremely. Wolverine's sense of smell is much sharper than that of an ordinary human.

vulnerable: Open to attack, undefended.

War Room: The room in Professor Xavier's School for Gifted Youngsters where the X-Men meet to make their plans to protect mutants and humans.

X-Men: A group of mutants brought together by Professor Charles Xavier. Their goal is to protect both humans and mutants from those mutants who would do them harm. They seek to promote peaceful coexistence between humans and mutants. They are sworn to protect a world that often fears and hates them. Led by Storm and Cyclops, the current membership includes Wolverine, Jubilee, Rogue, Gambit, and Jean Grey.